Questions lovingly answered by:

_________________________ & _________________________

How do I love thee? Let me count the ways.
I love thee to the depth and breadth and height
My soul can reach, when feeling out of sight
For the ends of being and ideal grace.
I love thee to the level of every day's
Most quiet need, by sun and candle-light.
I love thee freely, as men strive for right.
I love thee purely, as they turn from praise.
I love thee with the passion put to use
In my old griefs, and with my childhood's faith.
I love thee with a love I seemed to lose
With my lost saints. I love thee with the breath,
Smiles, tears, of all my life; and, if God choose,
I shall but love thee better after death.

— Elizabeth Barrett Browning —

Would you rather be with the cats or the dogs? Why?

☐ HER REPLY ☐ HIS REPLY

☐ HIS REPLY ☐ HER REPLY

What kind of person is your best friend?

☐ HER REPLY ☐ HIS REPLY

☐ HIS REPLY ☐ HER REPLY

What is the one thing you've learned about yourself?

☐ HER REPLY ☐ HIS REPLY

☐ HIS REPLY ☐ HER REPLY

Do you like the idea of having a boyfriend/girlfriend? Why?

☐ HER REPLY ☐ HIS REPLY

☐ HIS REPLY ☐ HER REPLY

What was something that your mother considered very important?

☐ HER REPLY ☐ HIS REPLY

☐ HIS REPLY ☐ HER REPLY

What is the most significant book you've read recently and why?

☐ HER REPLY ☐ HIS REPLY

☐ HIS REPLY ☐ HER REPLY

What is missing in your life?

☐ HER REPLY ☐ HIS REPLY   ☐ HIS REPLY ☐ HER REPLY

Why do you always have to explain what's wrong?

☐ HER REPLY ☐ HIS REPLY   ☐ HIS REPLY ☐ HER REPLY

Do you sometimes feel sorry for others? Why?

☐ HER REPLY ☐ HIS REPLY

☐ HIS REPLY ☐ HER REPLY

List of things that do not need to be hidden

☐ HER REPLY ☐ HIS REPLY

☐ HIS REPLY ☐ HER REPLY

What is the one thing that has made you interested in writing a book?

☐ HER REPLY ☐ HIS REPLY

☐ HIS REPLY ☐ HER REPLY

Do you love to make friends with children? Why?

☐ HER REPLY ☐ HIS REPLY

☐ HIS REPLY ☐ HER REPLY

What would you do if you suddenly discovered you didn't have a nose?

☐ HER REPLY ☐ HIS REPLY   ☐ HIS REPLY ☐ HER REPLY

What did I do during this moment and how would I go through it? How?

☐ HER REPLY ☐ HIS REPLY   ☐ HIS REPLY ☐ HER REPLY

What makes you feel sad or can easily drive you to desperation?

☐ HER REPLY ☐ HIS REPLY ☐ HIS REPLY ☐ HER REPLY

Who are your ideal role models?

☐ HER REPLY ☐ HIS REPLY ☐ HIS REPLY ☐ HER REPLY

When was the last time you had a great conversation with someone?

☐ HER REPLY ☐ HIS REPLY

☐ HIS REPLY ☐ HER REPLY

What is one thing you love about your country?

☐ HER REPLY ☐ HIS REPLY

☐ HIS REPLY ☐ HER REPLY

If you had to do nothing but work for a year, what would
you do? Why?

☐ HER REPLY   ☐ HIS REPLY   ☐ HIS REPLY   ☐ HER REPLY

What can you do to protect yourself from this?

☐ HER REPLY   ☐ HIS REPLY   ☐ HIS REPLY   ☐ HER REPLY

If you could be brave, would you and why?

☐ HER REPLY ☐ HIS REPLY

☐ HIS REPLY ☐ HER REPLY

What's the worst thing about being a parent?

☐ HER REPLY ☐ HIS REPLY

☐ HIS REPLY ☐ HER REPLY

What's your favorite holiday destination in a warm climate?

☐ HER REPLY ☐ HIS REPLY   ☐ HIS REPLY ☐ HER REPLY

How would you describe the feeling of being most important on your own?

☐ HER REPLY ☐ HIS REPLY   ☐ HIS REPLY ☐ HER REPLY

What one thing do you do now that you need an adult for but would like to try to do it all by yourself?

☐ HER REPLY ☐ HIS REPLY

☐ HIS REPLY ☐ HER REPLY

What is the one thing that makes you hate something?

☐ HER REPLY ☐ HIS REPLY

☐ HIS REPLY ☐ HER REPLY

List of things that can cause you excitement

☐ HER REPLY ☐ HIS REPLY   ☐ HIS REPLY ☐ HER REPLY

How do you deal with the fact that they aren't going to let you get in?

☐ HER REPLY ☐ HIS REPLY   ☐ HIS REPLY ☐ HER REPLY

What has changed and what hasn't?

☐ HER REPLY ☐ HIS REPLY   ☐ HIS REPLY ☐ HER REPLY

____________________________________   ____________________________________
____________________________________   ____________________________________
____________________________________   ____________________________________
____________________________________   ____________________________________
____________________________________   ____________________________________
____________________________________   ____________________________________
____________________________________   ____________________________________
____________________________________   ____________________________________

How do you stop your temper?

☐ HER REPLY ☐ HIS REPLY   ☐ HIS REPLY ☐ HER REPLY

____________________________________   ____________________________________
____________________________________   ____________________________________
____________________________________   ____________________________________
____________________________________   ____________________________________
____________________________________   ____________________________________
____________________________________   ____________________________________
____________________________________   ____________________________________

What changes would you be making that are important?

☐ HER REPLY ☐ HIS REPLY

☐ HIS REPLY ☐ HER REPLY

Which is more important to you, to let others know you are well or to always be there for them? Why?

☐ HER REPLY ☐ HIS REPLY

☐ HIS REPLY ☐ HER REPLY

Tell a story about the things that you think are important.

☐ HER REPLY ☐ HIS REPLY

☐ HIS REPLY ☐ HER REPLY

Am I creative? Why? Why not?

☐ HER REPLY ☐ HIS REPLY

☐ HIS REPLY ☐ HER REPLY

Why have you become complacent about what you are doing or feeling?

☐ HER REPLY ☐ HIS REPLY

☐ HIS REPLY ☐ HER REPLY

What is the one thing you won't do when you're on camera?

☐ HER REPLY ☐ HIS REPLY

☐ HIS REPLY ☐ HER REPLY

What's your least favorite regret?

☐ HER REPLY ☐ HIS REPLY ☐ HIS REPLY ☐ HER REPLY

What's the funniest thing you've heard?

☐ HER REPLY ☐ HIS REPLY ☐ HIS REPLY ☐ HER REPLY

What, if any, misconceptions about the mind do you have?

☐ HER REPLY ☐ HIS REPLY

☐ HIS REPLY ☐ HER REPLY

How did you help your children learn social skills?

☐ HER REPLY ☐ HIS REPLY

☐ HIS REPLY ☐ HER REPLY

Would you rather die young or live to 100?

☐ HER REPLY ☐ HIS REPLY

☐ HIS REPLY ☐ HER REPLY

Are you really that stupid? Why?

☐ HER REPLY ☐ HIS REPLY

☐ HIS REPLY ☐ HER REPLY

Do you have bad dreams? Describe those.

☐ HER REPLY ☐ HIS REPLY

☐ HIS REPLY ☐ HER REPLY

How do you keep your story interesting?

☐ HER REPLY ☐ HIS REPLY

☐ HIS REPLY ☐ HER REPLY

When you think you're happy, what's the first thing you think about?

☐ HER REPLY ☐ HIS REPLY

____

____

____

____

____

____

____

☐ HIS REPLY ☐ HER REPLY

____

____

____

____

____

____

____

If you could be any cartoon character, who would you be and why?

☐ HER REPLY ☐ HIS REPLY

____

____

____

____

____

____

____

☐ HIS REPLY ☐ HER REPLY

____

____

____

____

____

____

____

If you could be in the right place at the wrong time, which would you choose?

☐ HER REPLY ☐ HIS REPLY   ☐ HIS REPLY ☐ HER REPLY

____

Are you able to deal with situations with less friction? How?

☐ HER REPLY ☐ HIS REPLY   ☐ HIS REPLY ☐ HER REPLY

____

What are some of your worst habits?

☐ HER REPLY ☐ HIS REPLY

____

____

____

____

____

____

____

____

☐ HIS REPLY ☐ HER REPLY

____

____

____

____

____

____

____

____

What do we mean when they say, "You can catch more flies with honey than with vinegar"?

☐ HER REPLY ☐ HIS REPLY

____

____

____

____

____

____

____

____

☐ HIS REPLY ☐ HER REPLY

____

____

____

____

____

____

____

____

If you had to choose one thing to make a career change from, what would it be?

☐ HER REPLY ☐ HIS REPLY

☐ HIS REPLY ☐ HER REPLY

What's been your most awkward experience?

☐ HER REPLY ☐ HIS REPLY

☐ HIS REPLY ☐ HER REPLY

How would you describe the feeling of being lonely?

☐ HER REPLY ☐ HIS REPLY

☐ HIS REPLY ☐ HER REPLY

Do you think your life is hard? Why?

☐ HER REPLY ☐ HIS REPLY

☐ HIS REPLY ☐ HER REPLY

What are you looking forward to most next month?

☐ HER REPLY   ☐ HIS REPLY   ☐ HIS REPLY   ☐ HER REPLY

List of things that have happened

☐ HER REPLY   ☐ HIS REPLY   ☐ HIS REPLY   ☐ HER REPLY

What is the one thing you're always doing wrong?

☐ HER REPLY ☐ HIS REPLY   ☐ HIS REPLY ☐ HER REPLY

Why did you want to make a product that wouldn't sell?

☐ HER REPLY ☐ HIS REPLY   ☐ HIS REPLY ☐ HER REPLY

List of things that are impossible to get

☐ HER REPLY ☐ HIS REPLY

☐ HIS REPLY ☐ HER REPLY

If you could make one last phone call to someone before you die, who would you call and why? What are the things that you would say to the said person?

☐ HER REPLY ☐ HIS REPLY

☐ HIS REPLY ☐ HER REPLY

What is the one thing a human being will always accept when he/she goes to jail?

☐ HER REPLY ☐ HIS REPLY

☐ HIS REPLY ☐ HER REPLY

Would you ever engage in sexual intercourse if there was no right to do so? Why?

☐ HER REPLY ☐ HIS REPLY

☐ HIS REPLY ☐ HER REPLY

What's your favorite character to play?

☐ HER REPLY ☐ HIS REPLY

☐ HIS REPLY ☐ HER REPLY

Who would you trust to fight for your own interests?

☐ HER REPLY ☐ HIS REPLY

☐ HIS REPLY ☐ HER REPLY

What is one thing about your father that you don't like?

☐ HER REPLY ☐ HIS REPLY

☐ HIS REPLY ☐ HER REPLY

What can you do to learn from this?

☐ HER REPLY ☐ HIS REPLY

☐ HIS REPLY ☐ HER REPLY

What is the most significant problem facing the universe today?

☐ HER REPLY ☐ HIS REPLY   ☐ HIS REPLY ☐ HER REPLY

If you could choose between your health or your money, which would you choose and why?

☐ HER REPLY ☐ HIS REPLY   ☐ HIS REPLY ☐ HER REPLY

How do you help your children feel safe?

☐ HER REPLY ☐ HIS REPLY

____
____
____
____
____
____
____
____
____

☐ HIS REPLY ☐ HER REPLY

____
____
____
____
____
____
____
____
____

List of things that I've done after the exam

☐ HER REPLY ☐ HIS REPLY

____
____
____
____
____
____
____

☐ HIS REPLY ☐ HER REPLY

____
____
____
____
____
____
____

Describe the first time you ever danced with someone

☐ HER REPLY ☐ HIS REPLY

☐ HIS REPLY ☐ HER REPLY

What is one thing you have in common with the people that supported you in the past?

☐ HER REPLY ☐ HIS REPLY

☐ HIS REPLY ☐ HER REPLY

List of things that I'm not supposed to do

☐ HER REPLY ☐ HIS REPLY

☐ HIS REPLY ☐ HER REPLY

If your pet could talk, what's one thing they could say that would completely ruin your image?

☐ HER REPLY ☐ HIS REPLY

☐ HIS REPLY ☐ HER REPLY

Do you have a secret talent? Why or why not?

☐ HER REPLY   ☐ HIS REPLY

☐ HIS REPLY   ☐ HER REPLY

Who would you trust if you could not trust someone?

☐ HER REPLY   ☐ HIS REPLY

☐ HIS REPLY   ☐ HER REPLY

What makes you think it's not, or at least will take some time to be resolved?

☐ HER REPLY ☐ HIS REPLY

☐ HIS REPLY ☐ HER REPLY

List of things that are clearly and unequivocally wrong

☐ HER REPLY ☐ HIS REPLY

☐ HIS REPLY ☐ HER REPLY

If you could live with an alien, what would you do with it and why do you want to live with it?

☐ HER REPLY ☐ HIS REPLY   ☐ HIS REPLY ☐ HER REPLY

What is the most significant definition of the original purpose?

☐ HER REPLY ☐ HIS REPLY   ☐ HIS REPLY ☐ HER REPLY

What is the best thing you have ever done?

☐ HER REPLY ☐ HIS REPLY

☐ HIS REPLY ☐ HER REPLY

Would you rather live in the past or in the now?

☐ HER REPLY ☐ HIS REPLY

☐ HIS REPLY ☐ HER REPLY

What's a day of your life like?

☐ HER REPLY ☐ HIS REPLY

☐ HIS REPLY ☐ HER REPLY

How would you describe the feeling of being privileged?

☐ HER REPLY ☐ HIS REPLY

☐ HIS REPLY ☐ HER REPLY

Have you made any significant breakthroughs in the last few years that helped you or changed who you are?

☐ HER REPLY ☐ HIS REPLY   ☐ HIS REPLY ☐ HER REPLY

What is the most significant process you've had to overcome to improve your productivity?

☐ HER REPLY ☐ HIS REPLY   ☐ HIS REPLY ☐ HER REPLY

If you could ask one person to help you do what is hardest for you, who would it be?

☐ HER REPLY ☐ HIS REPLY

☐ HIS REPLY ☐ HER REPLY

What were you like when you were 16?

☐ HER REPLY ☐ HIS REPLY

☐ HIS REPLY ☐ HER REPLY

If your favorite animal was a dog and your least favorite animal was a cat, which would you pick?

☐ HER REPLY ☐ HIS REPLY

☐ HIS REPLY ☐ HER REPLY

What are you wearing now?

☐ HER REPLY ☐ HIS REPLY

☐ HIS REPLY ☐ HER REPLY

Do you think someone's lying to you right now? Why?

☐ HER REPLY ☐ HIS REPLY

☐ HIS REPLY ☐ HER REPLY

What is something you're scared of?

☐ HER REPLY ☐ HIS REPLY

☐ HIS REPLY ☐ HER REPLY

Do you always hate or do you love that you do not hate people who work for you?

☐ HER REPLY ☐ HIS REPLY

☐ HIS REPLY ☐ HER REPLY

What's the most important thing you want people to know about you?

☐ HER REPLY ☐ HIS REPLY

☐ HIS REPLY ☐ HER REPLY

How much is too much of anything?

☐ HER REPLY ☐ HIS REPLY

☐ HIS REPLY ☐ HER REPLY

Would you rather be alone for a few hours or longer?

☐ HER REPLY ☐ HIS REPLY

☐ HIS REPLY ☐ HER REPLY

What kind of TV commercial would you like to make? Describe it.

☐ HER REPLY ☐ HIS REPLY

☐ HIS REPLY ☐ HER REPLY

Would you break the law to save someone you love? Why?

☐ HER REPLY ☐ HIS REPLY

☐ HIS REPLY ☐ HER REPLY

What is one thing you can change if you could choose to do one thing over?

☐ HER REPLY ☐ HIS REPLY

☐ HIS REPLY ☐ HER REPLY

How would you describe the feeling of being young?

☐ HER REPLY ☐ HIS REPLY

☐ HIS REPLY ☐ HER REPLY

What qualities and acts do you have that make you the best character in the world?

☐ HER REPLY ☐ HIS REPLY

☐ HIS REPLY ☐ HER REPLY

What's your biggest pet peeve?

☐ HER REPLY ☐ HIS REPLY

☐ HIS REPLY ☐ HER REPLY

What are a few qualities you dislike in other people, and why?

☐ HER REPLY ☐ HIS REPLY

☐ HIS REPLY ☐ HER REPLY

List of things that are even more interesting

☐ HER REPLY ☐ HIS REPLY

☐ HIS REPLY ☐ HER REPLY

List of things that have inspired you

☐ HER REPLY ☐ HIS REPLY

☐ HIS REPLY ☐ HER REPLY

If someone handed you an envelope containing the exact date and time of your death, would you open it? Why or why not?

☐ HER REPLY ☐ HIS REPLY

☐ HIS REPLY ☐ HER REPLY

What is the one thing you do in the gym to motivate yourself?

☐ HER REPLY   ☐ HIS REPLY   ☐ HIS REPLY   ☐ HER REPLY

What are you reading? Who's your favorite author?

☐ HER REPLY   ☐ HIS REPLY   ☐ HIS REPLY   ☐ HER REPLY

Why are you up late more than most people having dark thoughts?

☐ HER REPLY ☐ HIS REPLY

____

☐ HIS REPLY ☐ HER REPLY

____

How do you stay calm and collected?

☐ HER REPLY ☐ HIS REPLY

____

☐ HIS REPLY ☐ HER REPLY

____

What's the most ridiculous thing you believe?

☐ HER REPLY ☐ HIS REPLY

☐ HIS REPLY ☐ HER REPLY

What are some things I really need?

☐ HER REPLY ☐ HIS REPLY

☐ HIS REPLY ☐ HER REPLY

What if you were asked to cry right now? What would you cry about?

☐ HER REPLY ☐ HIS REPLY

☐ HIS REPLY ☐ HER REPLY

What would the person you're talking to say about the day?

☐ HER REPLY ☐ HIS REPLY

☐ HIS REPLY ☐ HER REPLY

What are the top five things that irk you the most?

☐ HER REPLY ☐ HIS REPLY

☐ HIS REPLY ☐ HER REPLY

Who is the greatest performer of all time?

☐ HER REPLY ☐ HIS REPLY

☐ HIS REPLY ☐ HER REPLY

What is the one thing that you need right now that you just can't have right now?

☐ HER REPLY ☐ HIS REPLY   ☐ HIS REPLY ☐ HER REPLY

Does it bother you to be around someone who has bad manners? Why?

☐ HER REPLY ☐ HIS REPLY   ☐ HIS REPLY ☐ HER REPLY

What is the one thing you do not like about your workflow?

☐ HER REPLY ☐ HIS REPLY

☐ HIS REPLY ☐ HER REPLY

What makes you a good neighbor?

☐ HER REPLY ☐ HIS REPLY

☐ HIS REPLY ☐ HER REPLY

What if someone gives you $100.000? What would you do with it?

☐ HER REPLY ☐ HIS REPLY

☐ HIS REPLY ☐ HER REPLY

Discuss how conveniences change people's lives.

☐ HER REPLY ☐ HIS REPLY

☐ HIS REPLY ☐ HER REPLY

What would you do if you had four math problems marked wrong that were right?

☐ HER REPLY ☐ HIS REPLY

☐ HIS REPLY ☐ HER REPLY

Would you rather fight for the future that you've built or just let the old order crumble? Why?

☐ HER REPLY ☐ HIS REPLY

☐ HIS REPLY ☐ HER REPLY

What does your child want in a mother or a father?

☐ HER REPLY ☐ HIS REPLY

☐ HIS REPLY ☐ HER REPLY

What is the most heartwarming thing you've ever seen?

☐ HER REPLY ☐ HIS REPLY

☐ HIS REPLY ☐ HER REPLY

What is most important to you to be valued and appreciated?

☐ HER REPLY ☐ HIS REPLY   ☐ HIS REPLY ☐ HER REPLY

What's something people are surprised about?

☐ HER REPLY ☐ HIS REPLY   ☐ HIS REPLY ☐ HER REPLY

Why does the ocean have a tide?

☐ HER REPLY ☐ HIS REPLY   ☐ HIS REPLY ☐ HER REPLY

Why do you have this much money?

☐ HER REPLY ☐ HIS REPLY   ☐ HIS REPLY ☐ HER REPLY

Why is your happiness defined through the misery of someone else's happiness?

☐ HER REPLY ☐ HIS REPLY

☐ HIS REPLY ☐ HER REPLY

Which would you choose between an offense and a defense?

☐ HER REPLY ☐ HIS REPLY

☐ HIS REPLY ☐ HER REPLY

How would you describe the feeling of being on the wrong side of the truth?

☐ HER REPLY ☐ HIS REPLY

☐ HIS REPLY ☐ HER REPLY

If you could see yourself in another reality, what would you look like?

☐ HER REPLY ☐ HIS REPLY

☐ HIS REPLY ☐ HER REPLY

List of things that help your cats/dogs be calmer

☐ HER REPLY ☐ HIS REPLY

☐ HIS REPLY ☐ HER REPLY

What is the worst thing you have ever found?

☐ HER REPLY ☐ HIS REPLY

☐ HIS REPLY ☐ HER REPLY

How do you plan to spend your summer off? Do you plan to go camping or hiking?

☐ HER REPLY ☐ HIS REPLY

☐ HIS REPLY ☐ HER REPLY

If you could be anything you wanted to be, what would you be?

☐ HER REPLY ☐ HIS REPLY

☐ HIS REPLY ☐ HER REPLY

What is the proudest moment of your life?

☐ HER REPLY ☐ HIS REPLY

☐ HIS REPLY ☐ HER REPLY

What the hell are you thinking?

☐ HER REPLY ☐ HIS REPLY

☐ HIS REPLY ☐ HER REPLY

Tell about one of your mother—daughter/son activities.

☐ HER REPLY   ☐ HIS REPLY   ☐ HIS REPLY   ☐ HER REPLY

What do you value in a business deal?

☐ HER REPLY   ☐ HIS REPLY   ☐ HIS REPLY   ☐ HER REPLY

What if there is nothing, what will you do?

☐ HER REPLY ☐ HIS REPLY

____
____
____
____
____
____
____
____

☐ HIS REPLY ☐ HER REPLY

____
____
____
____
____
____
____
____

What are you trying to achieve?

☐ HER REPLY ☐ HIS REPLY

____
____
____
____
____
____

☐ HIS REPLY ☐ HER REPLY

____
____
____
____
____
____

What is one thing you have that the others don't?

☐ HER REPLY ☐ HIS REPLY

☐ HIS REPLY ☐ HER REPLY

If you had to choose one thing you're going to be doing in 5 years, what would that be?

☐ HER REPLY ☐ HIS REPLY

☐ HIS REPLY ☐ HER REPLY

Would you love to be in a movie with someone who likes you? Why?

☐ HER REPLY ☐ HIS REPLY

☐ HIS REPLY ☐ HER REPLY

Say something about what you've done and how you've done it.

☐ HER REPLY ☐ HIS REPLY

☐ HIS REPLY ☐ HER REPLY

What is the best thing to do when you find yourself regretting the choices you have made?

☐ HER REPLY ☐ HIS REPLY

☐ HIS REPLY ☐ HER REPLY

Favorite movie set in the '70s?

☐ HER REPLY ☐ HIS REPLY

☐ HIS REPLY ☐ HER REPLY

Do you ever have moments of anger? Do you have bad days? Why?

☐ HER REPLY ☐ HIS REPLY

☐ HIS REPLY ☐ HER REPLY

What do you like most about yourself?

☐ HER REPLY ☐ HIS REPLY

☐ HIS REPLY ☐ HER REPLY

What is the most surprising thing you have learned?

☐ HER REPLY   ☐ HIS REPLY

☐ HIS REPLY   ☐ HER REPLY

List of things that will drive me insane

☐ HER REPLY   ☐ HIS REPLY

☐ HIS REPLY   ☐ HER REPLY

How do you stop complaining and getting over it?

☐ HER REPLY ☐ HIS REPLY

____
____
____
____
____
____
____
____
____

☐ HIS REPLY ☐ HER REPLY

____
____
____
____
____
____
____
____
____

What is your worst quality?

☐ HER REPLY ☐ HIS REPLY

____
____
____
____
____
____
____

☐ HIS REPLY ☐ HER REPLY

____
____
____
____
____
____
____

What should you learn?

☐ HER REPLY ☐ HIS REPLY　　　　　☐ HIS REPLY ☐ HER REPLY

Would you rather be loved more or less or be hated more or less?

☐ HER REPLY ☐ HIS REPLY　　　　　☐ HIS REPLY ☐ HER REPLY

Do you ever forgive your father? Why?

What are you reading these days?

What is it that you are most thankful for?

☐ HER REPLY ☐ HIS REPLY   ☐ HIS REPLY ☐ HER REPLY

What sort of music would you like to hear?

☐ HER REPLY ☐ HIS REPLY   ☐ HIS REPLY ☐ HER REPLY

What does love look like?

□ HER REPLY □ HIS REPLY

□ HIS REPLY □ HER REPLY

What's your favorite thing to do as you travel abroad?

□ HER REPLY □ HIS REPLY

□ HIS REPLY □ HER REPLY

List of things that are shared across family members

☐ HER REPLY ☐ HIS REPLY

☐ HIS REPLY ☐ HER REPLY

Do you usually text or call more? Why?

☐ HER REPLY ☐ HIS REPLY

☐ HIS REPLY ☐ HER REPLY

What kind of pet would you most like to have? Why?

☐ HER REPLY ☐ HIS REPLY   ☐ HIS REPLY ☐ HER REPLY

How do you deal with a situation like that when you have the experience that you have?

☐ HER REPLY ☐ HIS REPLY   ☐ HIS REPLY ☐ HER REPLY

List of things that can kill you

☐ HER REPLY ☐ HIS REPLY

☐ HIS REPLY ☐ HER REPLY

What's the worst thing you've ever done as a person?

☐ HER REPLY ☐ HIS REPLY

☐ HIS REPLY ☐ HER REPLY

Do you need to be told when to break free and experiment
with your own path?

☐ HER REPLY   ☐ HIS REPLY   ☐ HIS REPLY   ☐ HER REPLY

If you had to choose your five favorite sports players, who
would they be?

☐ HER REPLY   ☐ HIS REPLY   ☐ HIS REPLY   ☐ HER REPLY

If you could make a movie about your childhood to be done in 12 days, what would it be?

☐ HER REPLY ☐ HIS REPLY

☐ HIS REPLY ☐ HER REPLY

The wind was harsh and violent. The wind… [continue the sentence]

☐ HER REPLY ☐ HIS REPLY

☐ HIS REPLY ☐ HER REPLY

What is one thing that you wish you could have done?

☐ HER REPLY ☐ HIS REPLY

____
____
____
____
____
____
____
____
____

☐ HIS REPLY ☐ HER REPLY

____
____
____
____
____
____
____
____
____

When was the last time you ever felt joyous?

☐ HER REPLY ☐ HIS REPLY

____
____
____
____
____
____
____

☐ HIS REPLY ☐ HER REPLY

____
____
____
____
____
____
____

What is the most difficult part of being a (insert your job)?

☐ HER REPLY ☐ HIS REPLY

____
____
____
____
____
____
____
____

☐ HIS REPLY ☐ HER REPLY

____
____
____
____
____
____
____
____

Can you just go with it? Why?

☐ HER REPLY ☐ HIS REPLY

____
____
____
____
____
____
____
____

☐ HIS REPLY ☐ HER REPLY

____
____
____
____
____
____
____
____

How do you deal with fear?

☐ HER REPLY ☐ HIS REPLY   ☐ HIS REPLY ☐ HER REPLY

How many things do you have in this life?

☐ HER REPLY ☐ HIS REPLY   ☐ HIS REPLY ☐ HER REPLY

How would you describe the feeling of being scared that what you are doing is wrong?

☐ HER REPLY ☐ HIS REPLY   ☐ HIS REPLY ☐ HER REPLY

What can you do to make you feel better about what happened?

☐ HER REPLY ☐ HIS REPLY   ☐ HIS REPLY ☐ HER REPLY

What activity calms you down and makes you feel at peace with the world?

☐ HER REPLY ☐ HIS REPLY

☐ HIS REPLY ☐ HER REPLY

Who has impressed you most with what they've accomplished?

☐ HER REPLY ☐ HIS REPLY

☐ HIS REPLY ☐ HER REPLY

Does the lifestyle you want for you and your loved ones align with what you think is right for you right now?

☐ HER REPLY ☐ HIS REPLY

☐ HIS REPLY ☐ HER REPLY

What do you need to be careful of?

☐ HER REPLY ☐ HIS REPLY

☐ HIS REPLY ☐ HER REPLY

How would you describe the feeling of being together in such a difficult time with someone you really loved?

☐ HER REPLY ☐ HIS REPLY

☐ HIS REPLY ☐ HER REPLY

What would you choose instead of sex?

☐ HER REPLY ☐ HIS REPLY

☐ HIS REPLY ☐ HER REPLY

Do you have a quick and easy excuse? Why?

□ HER REPLY □ HIS REPLY

□ HIS REPLY □ HER REPLY

If you were to live the rest of your life again, what would you do differently?

□ HER REPLY □ HIS REPLY

□ HIS REPLY □ HER REPLY

If you could pick one thing from your childhood to take with you into adulthood, what would it be?

☐ HER REPLY ☐ HIS REPLY

☐ HIS REPLY ☐ HER REPLY

So what are you waiting for? Be free or stay stuck?

☐ HER REPLY ☐ HIS REPLY

☐ HIS REPLY ☐ HER REPLY

How would you describe the feeling of being dumped?

☐ HER REPLY ☐ HIS REPLY

☐ HIS REPLY ☐ HER REPLY

What have you done that has surprised you?

☐ HER REPLY ☐ HIS REPLY

☐ HIS REPLY ☐ HER REPLY

What is most often cited as the reason why women have to be
silent in church?

☐ HER REPLY   ☐ HIS REPLY

☐ HIS REPLY   ☐ HER REPLY

____

____

____

____

____

____

____

What if you're left in an island alone and you could only bring
3 things with you, what would you bring and why?

☐ HER REPLY   ☐ HIS REPLY

☐ HIS REPLY   ☐ HER REPLY

____

____

____

____

____

____

What is one thing you as a superhero fan cannot live without?

☐ HER REPLY ☐ HIS REPLY   ☐ HIS REPLY ☐ HER REPLY

When have you felt your biggest adrenaline rush?

☐ HER REPLY ☐ HIS REPLY   ☐ HIS REPLY ☐ HER REPLY

What are some of the nicknames you have for customers or coworkers?

☐ HER REPLY ☐ HIS REPLY

☐ HIS REPLY ☐ HER REPLY

Which are the best and worst ways of making your life?

☐ HER REPLY ☐ HIS REPLY

☐ HIS REPLY ☐ HER REPLY